Calm Ninja
ACTIVITY BOOK

Ninja Life Hacks™

Welcome

Hi there, ninjas! I'm Calm Ninja and this is my activity book. It's packed with puzzles, games, and brilliant tips to help you stay cool and calm.

This book belongs to

....
....

Join me and my friends for some super-chilled fill-in fun!

NEED SOME 'ME' TIME?

Just pick up this book to discover lots of awesome ways to hack into your inner calm. As well as lots of fun activities to complete, you'll find helpful relaxation techniques and breathing exercises to try out, plus mindful mazes and things to do, to help you manage big feelings and make life more chill!

Contents

ALL ABOUT ME!

Choose your favorite pens and pencils, then fill in these pages all about you!

My name is ....

My birthday is on ....

I am .... years old

I live with ....

My hometown is

....

My school is

....

Draw a circle around the 3 words that describe you best:

QUIET   SHY   FUNNY   STRESSED

CALM   DREAMY   CREATIVE   KIND

ANXIOUS   GRUMPY   LONELY

SAD   HARD-WORKING   ANXIOUS

What do you prefer?

(YOU CAN ONLY CIRCLE ONE!)

BEING IN A CROWD
or
BEING ON YOUR OWN

PAJAMAS or FANCY CLOTHES

PARTY or QUIET NIGHT IN

LOTS OF NOISE or SILENCE

BOOKS or MOVIES

POPCORN or CHIPS

DAY IN BED or NATURE WALK

RUNNING SHOES or SLIPPERS

TALKING or LISTENING

My best
friends are . . .

....

....

....

If I were an animal I would be a:

....

If I were a tree I would be a:

....

Ninja Life Hacks™

All about me!

The three CALMEST people I know:

....

....

....

The three most STRESSED people I know:

....

....

....

My favorite way to chill out is:

DRAW A PICTURE

GO FOR A RUN

READ A BOOK

PLAY WITH MY PET

Check your top choice!

TAKE A BUBBLE BATH

LEARN A NEW SKILL

LISTEN TO MUSIC

OTHER:

....

....

**DRAW A PICTURE OF
YOURSELF CHILLING OUT HERE**

WE ARE ALL DIFFERENT!
EVERYONE FINDS
DIFFERENT THINGS
RELAXING!

All about me!

Check the things you like to do in your spare time!

- ☐ Painting or drawing
- ☐ Listening to or playing music
- ☐ Sports
- ☐ Cooking something delicious
- ☐ Hanging out with friends
- ☐ Playing video games
- ☐ Other ....

Check the things that make you feel stressed:

- ☐ Lots of homework
- ☐ Being late
- ☐ Fighting with friends
- ☐ Losing something
- ☐ Having an argument with your family
- ☐ Not being listened to
- ☐ Other ....

Draw pictures or write in
the thought bubbles below!

I am really good at . . .

Today I am feeling . . .

My favorite animal is . . .

The best time of year is . . .

When I grow
up I want to be . . .

GO WITH THE FLOW!

Calm Ninja and friends are doing some calming yoga exercises. Can you put the jumbled-up picture back together?

A B C D E F

Write the letters in the correct order here:

DE-STRESS!

Zen Ninja wants to share some useful strategies to help you relax when you feel stressed. Color in each one as you try it out.

Look through happy photos

Take a bubble bath

PUT SMILEY FACE STICKERS NEXT TO THE THREE THINGS THAT WORK THE BEST FOR YOU.

Paint a picture

Cuddle your pet

Go for a walk

Write yourself positive messages and stick them around your room

Call a friend

Play a game of cards

Listen to music

Read a book

What else could you do to de-stress?

....

....

Worry Ninja

Zen Ninja

WORD SEARCH

There are ten calming words hidden in this word search. Can you help Frustrated Ninja to find them all?

Take your time and enjoy it—there's no hurry!

Check off each word when you find it in the grid.

D	E	T	U	J	M	H	N	H	B	K	O
F	R	R	Y	G	E	S	E	R	E	N	E
E	E	G	T	M	P	G	Z	O	U	G	H
P	L	A	E	R	E	W	A	R	M	S	W
G	A	B	I	W	A	G	Z	G	U	O	G
W	X	L	U	G	C	N	M	H	P	I	U
E	E	L	Q	O	E	G	Q	G	I	V	P
M	D	I	A	X	F	A	B	U	X	R	W
O	G	H	F	P	U	P	R	G	I	G	F
F	B	C	O	O	L	G	S	T	I	L	L
W	U	O	E	M	B	E	I	G	E	U	X
A	G	I	D	C	H	G	J	L	G	V	F

- ☐ RELAXED
- ☐ CHILL
- ☐ PEACEFUL
- ☐ QUIET
- ☐ HUSH
- ☐ STILL
- ☐ TRANQUIL
- ☐ SERENE
- ☐ ZEN
- ☐ COOL

How did this activity make YOU feel?

Add a thumbs-up or a thumbs-down sticker here.

13

MY CALM KIT!

Create your very own 'calm kit' to banish anxious feelings when they threaten to take over. Just open up your kit and enter . . . the calm zone!

YOU WILL NEED:

- [ ] A big cardboard box
- [ ] Some paper and coloring pens
- [ ] Glue or tape
- [ ] A selection of items to put in your box

ASK A GROWN-UP TO HELP YOU.

Here are some ideas for things to put in your box, but you can choose anything you like!

JOURNAL

BLANKET

TOYS

PILLOW

PENS AND PAPER

SOME FUNNY JOKES

PUZZLES

STRESS BALL

I'm Calm Ninja! I've got all my favorite things in my calm kit!

MY SPECIAL CALM KIT

BOOKS

FIDGET TOY

PHOTOS OF YOUR FAVORITE PEOPLE

Cut out or copy this label onto a piece of paper, then color it in using calming shades and patterns.

Now stick the label on your box and fill it up!

How did this activity make YOU feel?

Add a thumbs-up or a thumbs-down sticker here.

SKIP IT OUT!

Healthy Ninja knows that exercise is the perfect way to de-stress when feeling uptight. It gets rid of lots of pent-up negative feelings!

I just skip it out! It always helps me feel better!

USE YOUR STICKERS TO ADD BIRDS, BEES, AND OTHER CREATURES TO THE SCENE.

WOODLAND WANDER

When life gets too busy, Calm Ninja goes for a peaceful nature walk with friends.

Help the ninjas find their way through the trees, spotting all the things in the panel below on the way.

START HERE

Check off each one as you pass it.

- ☐ RED BUTTERFLY
- ☐ BLUE BIRD
- ☐ PINK FLOWERS
- ☐ HEDGEHOG
- ☐ BEES
- ☐ PURPLE BUTTERFLY
- ☐ RABBIT
- ☐ ORANGE FLOWERS

LOOK FOR THE ITEMS IN THE ORDER LISTED TO FIND THE RIGHT WAY!

FINISH

Ah! Peace and quiet at last!

How did this activity make YOU feel?

Add a thumbs-up or a thumbs-down sticker here.

19

BUTTERFLY BREATHING

Calm Ninja knows that slow and steady breathing can help you to stay calm when you start to feel anxious. Try out this breathing technique next time your heart starts to race!

Start with your finger on the butterfly, then follow the dotted line!

BREATHE IN

BREATHE OUT

Imagine that you are a butterfly, flitting from flower to flower. Trace the dotted lines with your finger, breathing in and out slowly as you move between them.

BREATHE IN

BREATHE IN

BREATHE OUT

BREATHE OUT

FILL-IN FUN

Fill in a word on each line to complete the story. Remember, it's your story, so you decide what happens!

One day .... Ninja was feeling ....
(name) (negative feeling)

"Why don't you play .... with me?"
(fun game)

suggested Calm Ninja. The two ninja played until they

were very .... Then they decided to
(feeling)

make lots of .... to eat. "Now, let's take
(favorite food)

the .... for a walk!" said Calm Ninja.
(pet)

On the way, they saw lots of .... flowers and
(color)

beautiful .... "What a .... day!"
(anything you like!) (descriptive word)

said .... Ninja.
(name)

"I feel .... now!"
(positive feeling)

How did this activity make YOU feel?

Add a thumbs-up or a thumbs-down sticker here.

ESCAPE YOUR WORRIES

Send your stress and anxiety sailing away by focusing on this calming coloring activity.

Take your time coloring in this picture and enjoy the process.

CLOSE YOUR EYES AND IMAGINE THE SOUNDS AND SMELLS OF THE SEASIDE. CAN YOU HEAR THE RIPPLING WAVES OR THE SQUAWKS OF SEA BIRDS? MAYBE YOU CAN SMELL THE SALTY AIR.

Use as many different colors as you can to shade some fabulous fish scales.

Calm Ninja, Zen Ninja, and Grateful Ninja are taking time out of their busy day to enjoy a relaxing walk in the mountains.

Being outdoors always makes them feel calm and happy.

3 x PURPLE BUTTERFLIES	5 x RED POPPIES	3 x TORTOISES	4 x ORANGE BIRDS

Can you help the friends spot all these things? Check off each item with a Ninja sticker when you have found them all.

TWO ITEMS IN THE LIST ARE MISSING FROM THE BIG PICTURE. USE YOUR STICKERS TO ADD THEM IN.

1 x BIRD'S NEST	5 x BLUEBIRDS	1 x CLOUD (SHAPED LIKE A FISH)	2 x RABBITS

A MANTRA A DAY!

A mantra a day keeps worries at bay! Choose one mantra for each day of the week from the list on the opposite page then fill in the planner with your choices Say your daily mantras out loud wheneve you feel anxious or worried.

TO DO THIS WEEK!

WEEK STARTING: ..../........./..........

MONDAY	
TUESDAY	
WEDNESDAY	
THURSDAY	
FRIDAY	
SATURDAY	
SUNDAY	

I give myself permission to relax!

Be kind to yourself!

Listen to your body!

Take one day at a time!

I do not need to be perfect!

Breathe in, breathe out . . .

I am proud of myself for trying!

You can come up with your own mantras, too!

It is ok to take a break!

I am good enough as I am!

I accept myself as I am!

STICK THE PLANNER UP ON A WALL WHERE YOU CAN SEE IT EVERY DAY!

How did this activity make YOU feel?

Add a thumbs-up or a thumbs-down sticker here.

CALMING COLORS

Did you know that different colors can change your mood? Shade in the fishes in each tank using the color keys at the bottom of the page.

HOT COLOR KEY 1 ● 2 ● 3 ● 4 ●

COOL COLOR KEY

5 ● 6 ● 7 ● 8 ●

Watching fish always makes me feel super-calm!

WHEN YOU ARE DONE, ADD A CALM NINJA ICON STICKER NEXT TO THE PICTURE THAT MAKES YOU FEEL THE MOST RELAXED.

CLEAN UP!

Can you help clean up Organized Ninja's bedroom and organize the items?

Draw a red circle around all the sports equipment, a blue circle around the art items, and a green circle around digital devices.

Thanks for the help! Cleaning up helps me feel calm and on top of things!

Now help Organized Ninja put all these books in the order from smallest to biggest.

Number each book, with 1 as the smallest and 7 as the largest.

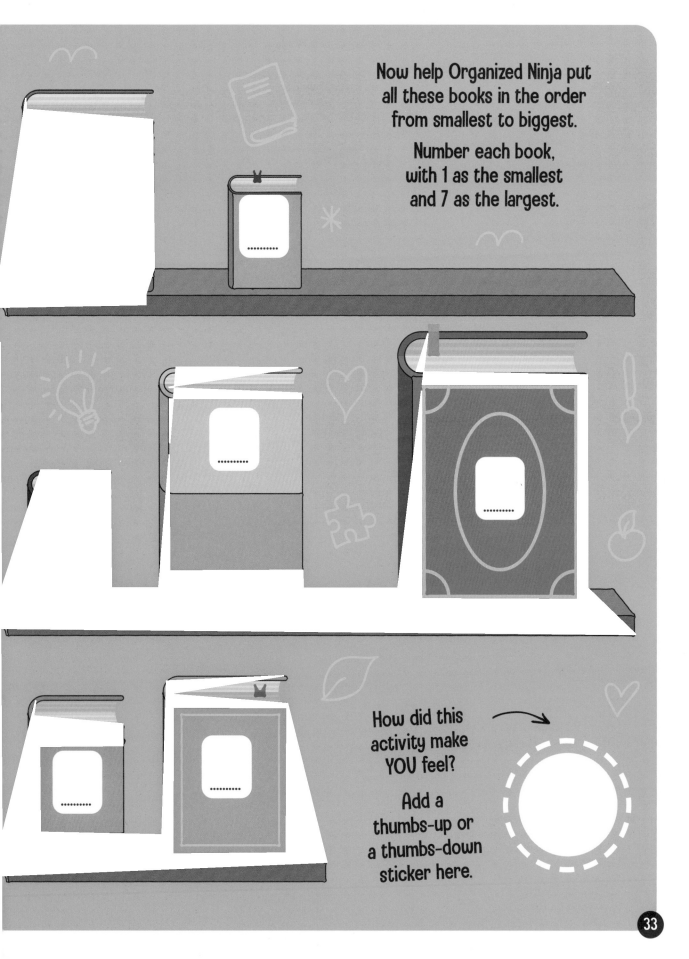

How did this activity make YOU feel?

Add a thumbs-up or a thumbs-down sticker here.

CHILL OUT!

Doing a coloring activity is a brilliant way to discover your inner calm—so choose your favorite pens and pencils and get creative with this chill poster.

PEACE AT LAST!

Calm Ninja and Grateful Ninja are relaxing in a peaceful place—but where are they? Connect the dots to find out, then add emblem stickers to their chests and color in the scene.

SUDOKU

Doing fun puzzles can help to occupy your brain when you are feeling anxious, so you can put your worries to one side for a while.

Try this sudoku challenge with Worry Ninja!

There should only be one of each flower in every row, column, and small square.

Doing puzzles helps me to forget my worries!

A

B

C

D

CALM DOS AND DON'TS

We all get angry sometimes, but if you know what to do—and what NOT to do—when anger threatens to take over, it will stop things from getting out of hand.

DON'Ts!

Put a cross next to the DON'Ts that YOU need to avoid the most.

- ☐ Shout at someone
- ☐ Kick or hit
- ☐ Blame others
- ☐ Refuse to listen
- ☐ Call people names
- ☐ Threaten
- ☐ Break things

DOs!

Put a cross next to the DOs that YOU find most helpful.

- ☐ Listen to what others have to say
- ☐ Explain what you feel
- ☐ Show respect
- ☐ Talk it out
- ☐ Walk away until you are calm
- ☐ Read a book or listen to music to relax
- ☐ Ask for help

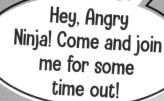

I feel so angry, I'm going to explode!

Hey, Angry Ninja! Come and join me for some time out!

HUG IT OUT!

Offering a hug is a great way to say you are sorry and restore peace after an argument.

Color in this heartfelt apology, then add more heart stickers to show the love!

MY CALM PLACE

Where is Calm Ninja's favorite place to go to relax? Follow the tangled strings to find out.

A

B

C

My favorite place always makes me feel calm and happy!

What's your favorite calm place?

....

TAKE A BREAK!

Everyone needs a break once and a while.

If you feel anxious, upset, or stressed, take some time out and use this calm chart to award yourself a break. Just pick an activity and color in the star when you have tried it.

 Jump to the beat of a song

 WATCH FISH

 Count backwards from 100

 TAKE A BATH

 Chat with a friend

 WRITE A POEM

 Look at happy photos

Cuddle a pet	STRETCH!		Slow your breathing
WRITE A LETTER	Do a handstand	HUG SOMEONE	Count your heartbeats
	Have a cool drink	SING OUT LOUD	Paint a picture

CAN YOU THINK OF ANY OTHER THINGS YOU COULD DO? WRITE YOUR OWN IDEAS IN THE EMPTY SPACES.

Sad Ninja

I feel so sad today . . .

Pick an activity! Doing fun things always helps me!

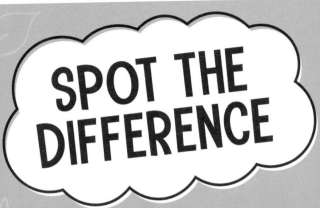

SPOT THE DIFFERENCE

Can you spot eight differences between these pictures of Calm Ninja, Focused Ninja, and Zen Ninja doing yoga?

Add a star sticker or color in a circle below for every difference you spot.

Add a star sticker in the circles below for every difference you spot.

ALSO KNOWN AS . . .

Calm Ninja's friends have a special name for their super-chill pal. Can you crack the code to work out Calm Ninja's nickname?

Each symbol represents a letter. Use the key to help you work out the answer!

HOW TO DECODE THE MESSAGE:

● = A   ▬ = K   ⬠ = O

■ = C   ⬡ = L   ▼ = S

▲ = E   ◣ = M   ◖ = Y

★ = I   ◆ = N

ONE CHILL NINJA!

Draw in the missing squares to complete the picture of Calm Ninja, then color it in.

SOOTHING WORDS

Unscramble these letter wheels to reveal five soothing words.

The letter in the middle is the first letter of each word.

A
....

B
....

C
....

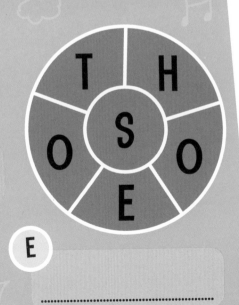

D
....

E
....

MAKE IT MATCH!

Listening to the sounds of nature always helps Stressed Ninja to relax! Color in the missing parts of each picture and use your stickers to make them match.

What are your favorite sounds in nature?

49

FISHY FUN

Calm Ninja loves to watch fish at the aquarium. It's so relaxing! Can you help him spot his favorite fish in the tank?

My favorite fish is red with yellow fins and a green tail.

How did this activity make YOU feel?

Add a thumbs-up or a thumbs-down sticker here.

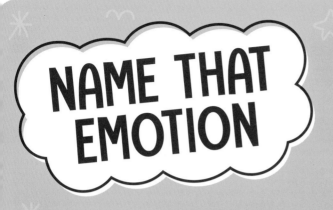

NAME THAT EMOTION

If you learn to recognize different emotions it will help you figure out how to handle them and restore calm.

Draw lines to help match each ninja with the correct emotion.

CALM

ANGRY

JEALOUS

SAD

LONELY

ANXIOUS

51

5, 4, 3, 2, 1!

When big emotions threaten to take over, use this technique to ground you and stay calm.

YOU CAN USE THIS TECHNIQUE AT ANY TIME, WHEREVER YOU ARE!

Use your five sense to help you describe . . .

5 objects
you can see right now.

....

....

....

....

....

3 things
you can hear right now.

....

....

....

2 things
you can smell right now.

....

....

1 thing
you can taste right now.

....

This technique helps me to feel present in my body and my mind!

How did this activity make YOU feel?

Add a thumbs-up or a thumbs-down sticker here.

MAKE A PINWHEEL

What could be more relaxing than watching a pinwheel turning in the breeze? Follow these simple instructions to make your very own.

YOU WILL NEED:

- [ ] 2 craft paper squares in different colors 8 in x 8 in
- [ ] Paper pin fasteners
- [ ] Pencil with a point
- [ ] Ruler
- [ ] A Straw
- [ ] Putty
- [ ] Scissors

ASK A GROWN-UP TO HELP YOU.

HOW TO MAKE IT:

1. Stick two different colored squares of craft paper together.

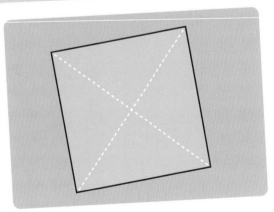

2. Fold the square into quarters, corner to corner, as shown above, then open the square and lay it down flat.

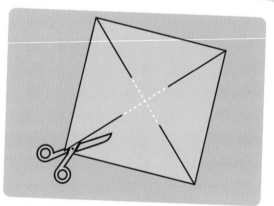

3. Cut in about two-thirds of the way along each fold line. Do NOT cut all the way to the center.

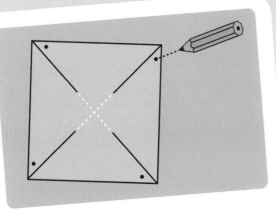

4. Using a pointed pencil, make a hole on the 4 flaps, in the positions shown.

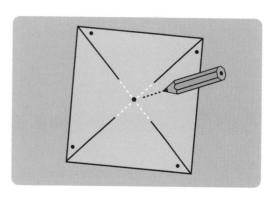

5. Poke a hole in the center and wiggle the pencil to widen it.

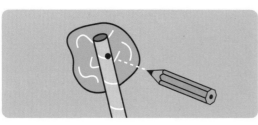

6. Place the putty behind the straw. Then, ask a grownup to make a hole in the top of the straw with a sharp tool, then use the pencil to widen it. Stick the center hole of the craft paper on to the putty. The hole in the straw and the paper should line up.

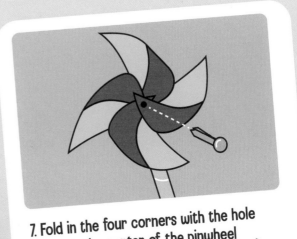

7. Fold in the four corners with the hole towards the center of the pinwheel and put a paper fastener through the middle.

8. Push the paper fastener through the hole in the straw and open out. Your pinwheel is ready to use!

DOT-TO-DOT

Calm Ninja knows that starting your morning with yoga sets you up for a chill day ahead!

HERE'S A CLUE—IT'S NAMED AFTER A SNAKE.

Connect the dots to discover which awesome yoga pose this is.

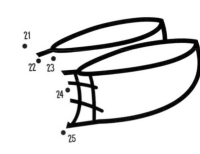

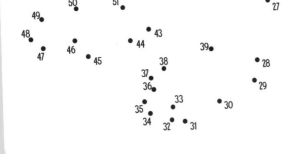
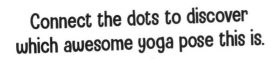

VISUALIZE IT!

Visiting a peaceful place in your mind is a great way to reduce your stress levels.

Make yourself comfortable, then close your eyes and picture a calm, tranquil scene . . .

How does it smell?

How does it look?

How does it feel to be there?

What can you hear?

Draw your scene here.

Think about these questions as you visualize the scene!

CREATING CALM

Why not create your very own 'calm mood board'?

Just arrange lots of random items that make you feel calm on a large piece of board, then stick them in place.

YOU WILL NEED:

- [ ] A large piece of cardboard
  (maybe the side of a large cardboard box)
- [ ] Scissors
- [ ] Glue
- [ ] Magazines
- [ ] Photographs
- [ ] Things that make you feel calm
- [ ] Pens and colored pencils

ASK A GROWN-UP TO HELP YOU.

Ideas for your mood board:

PICTURES

WORDS

SONG LYRICS

PIECES OF ART

TRAVEL DESTINATIONS

PHOTOS

SOFT FABRICS

WHEN YOU'VE MADE YOUR BOARD, STICK IT UP ON YOUR WALL. LOOK AT YOUR MOOD BOARD AND FEEL THOSE CALM VIBES ANY TIME YOU LIKE!

CALM MANTRAS

PATTERNS

PHOTOS OF YOUR FAVORITE PEOPLE

WHAT'S YOUR THING?

Follow the tangled lines to discover each ninja's favorite calming activity.

Angry Ninja

Calm Ninja

Listening Ninja

A

B

C

What's your favorite calming activity?

Grateful Ninja

CALM COLORING

Color the three things that make you feel most calm in your favorite shades.

How did this activity make YOU feel?

Add a thumbs-up or a thumbs-down sticker here.

FROM YOU TO I

Blaming others when things go wrong usually makes things worse. To avoid blame and keep things calm, try this clever technique . . .

All you need to do is change your sentences to start with 'I' instead of 'you.'

For example, don't say . . .

Instead, you could say . . .

You are mean! You tripped me up on purpose.

I am upset because you tripped me up!

Angry Ninja

Forgetful Ninja

Practice makes perfect! Draw lines to match
up these sentences to a better alternative.

You are
copying my work!
Stop it!

Let's play fair.

You cut in line.
Get out of
the way!

I don't want
anyone to copy
my work.

You always
cheat!

I think I was
here first.

You are really
annoying!

I would like
you to listen to
what I say!

You stole
my candy!

I am upset
with you.

You are not
listening to me!

I can't find my
candy! Have you
seen them?

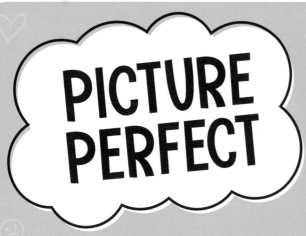

PICTURE PERFECT

Anxious Ninja is doing a lovely calm activity. Find the missing sticker pieces, then add them to the spaces to complete the picture and find out what it is.

JUST ONE THING...

If you know what to do when BIG feelings start to take over, it will help you to get the situation under control.

Write down one thing you can do to stay calm in these situations.

When I am angry I can ....

....

When I am nervous I can..

....

When I am stressed I can ....

....

When I am impatient I can..

....

Being prepared is your secret ninja superpower!

How did this activity make YOU feel?

Add a thumbs-up or a thumbs-down sticker here.

WORD POWER!

Calm Ninja has written the word "peaceful" on the board. Can you think of a calming word or sentence that starts with each of the letters?

P

E

A

C

E

F

U

L

HERE'S AN EXAMPLE TO GET YOU STARTED!

P eace and quiet

MATCH UP!

Frustrated Ninja is trying to find the two pictures of Calm Ninja that are exactly the same. Can you help?

JUST FOR YOU!

Kind Ninja loves to bake delicious snacks for the other ninjas—and it's relaxing, too! Color in cupcakes in lots of delicious flavors, using the color key below to give these treats a sweet flavor!

Anyone for a yummy treat?

COLOR KEY

● strawberry   ● blackberry

○ banana   ○ blueberry

THE BIG SQUEEZE!

If your body feels tense and uptight, try this exercise to relax your muscles.

1, 2, 3, 4, 5 . . .

WHAT TO DO!

1. Lie flat on your back, somewhere comfortable.

2. Starting with your toes, squeeze the muscles in them tightly.

3. Count to five, then release the muscles, paying attention to how your body feels.

4. Repeat by moving up the body and squeezing different muscles, one at a time.

5. When you have worked your way to the top of your head, lie still for a moment or two.

CALM-O-METER

Different calming strategies work for different people. Try out the ideas in the calm-o-meter below.

Patient Ninja — **Count to ten**

Gritty Ninja — **Exercise**

Zen Ninja — **Do some yoga**

Anxious Ninja — **Take a walk**

Angry Ninja — **Listen to music**

Positive Ninja — **Say a positive mantra out loud**

After you try each calming strategy, color in the face
to reflect how you feel about the activity.

CALM CATERPILLARS

Create two cool, calm caterpillars by filling each missing part of the bodies with a calming strategy on the page. Use it to help you when you feel stressed or anxious.

Hug a toy

Go for a walk

Do yoga

Have a cold drink

Visualize a calm place

Count to ten

Sing a song

Take a deep breath

Squeeze a stress ball

Take a break

Ask for help

You can add in your own ideas too!

73

COUNT YOUR HEARTBEAT!

Your heartbeat is the number of times your heart beats in one minute.

Making your heart beat faster when you do exercise is good for you, but it can also speed up when you get stressed or anxious, too—and this can feel very unpleasant!

Follow these steps to count your normal, resting heartbeat.

YOU WILL NEED:

- ☐ A stopwatch
- ☐ A pen
- ☐ Some paper

1. Relax for ten minutes, so you are calm.

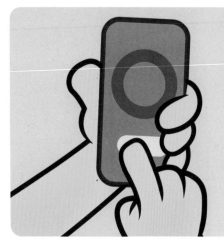

2. Set the stopwatch for 60 seconds.

3. Place two fingers on your wrist, just beneath your thumb.

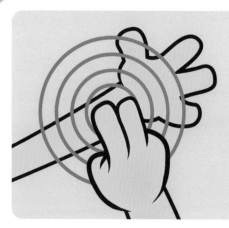

4. Apply gentle pressure until you can feel the beat, then press start on the stopwatch.

5. Count the number of beats you feel in 60 seconds.
This is your resting heartbeat.

IF YOUR HEART IS RACING, TRY OUT A STRATEGY FROM YOUR CALM CATERPILLARS (PAGES 72 AND 73). IT WILL HELP YOU TO CHILL AND SLOW YOUR HEARTBEAT DOWN AGAIN.

When at rest, the average heartbeat for a kid is between 55 and 85 beats per minute.

How did this activity make YOU feel?

Add a thumbs-up or a thumbs-down sticker here.

WHAT NEXT?

Calm Ninja always feels more peaceful when things are in the right order. Can you help by working out what comes next in each row?

CIRCLE WHAT COMES NEXT IN EACH SEQUENCE!

I love organizing things!

WIND DOWN...

Try out these activities before bedtime to help you wind down and get a relaxing night's sleep. Use your stickers to rank each activity from 1 to 5, with 1 being the most useful.

- [ ] Listening to soothing music

- [ ] Stargazing

- [ ] Reading a book

A good night's sleep will help you to cope with your day!

- [ ] Coloring a picture

- [ ] Taking a bath

SHADOW MATCH

Calm Ninja is reading a book to wind down before bedtime. Which shadow is an exact match with the big picture?

MINDFUL COLORING!

Focusing on an absorbing task can free your mind from worries! Color in this intricate pattern with your favorite colors and just chill.

Answers:

PAGE 10: ODD ONE OUT

PAGE 11: GO WITH THE FLOW
E, C, B, F, A, D

PAGE 13: WORD SEARCH

D	E	T	U	J	M	H	N	H	B	K	O
F	R	R	Y	G	E	S	E	R	E	N	E
E	E	G	T	M	P	G	Z	O	U	G	H
P	L	A	E	R	E	W	A	R	M	S	W
G	A	B	I	W	A	Z	G	U	O	G	
W	X	L	U	G	C	N	M	H	P	I	U
E	E	L	Q	O	E	G	Q	G	I	V	P
M	D	I	A	X	F	A	B	U	X	R	W
O	G	H	F	P	U	P	R	G	I	G	F
F	B	C	O	O	L	G	S	T	I	L	L
W	U	O	E	M	B	E	I	G	E	U	X
A	G	I	D	C	H	G	J	L	G	V	F

PAGE 16: CAN YOU SPOT IT

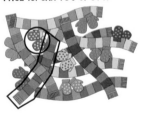

PAGES 18-19: WOODLAND WANDER

PAGES 22-23: MIRROR MATCH

PAGES 26-27: NURTURING NATURE!

PAGES 32-33: CLEAN UP!

PAGE 35: PEACE AT LAST!

PAGE 36: SUDOKU

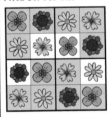

PAGE 39: MY CALM PLACE
ANSWER IS C

PAGES 42-43: SPOT THE DIFFERENCE

PAGE 44: ALSO KNOWN AS...
MY NICKNAME IS COOLIO

PAGE 46: FOLLOW THE MUSIC

PAGE 47: SOOTHING WORDS
A: REST. B: RELAX. C: QUIET. D: STILL. E: SOOTHE

PAGE 50: FISHY FUN

PAGE 51: NAME THAT EMOTION

PAGE 56: DOT-TO-DOT

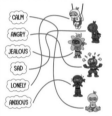

PAGE 60: WHAT'S YOUR THING?
ANGRY NINJA: B. CALM NINJA: A. LISTENING NINJA: C.

PAGES 62-63: FROM YOU TO I

PAGE 67: MATCH UP
F AND I ARE EXACTLY THE SAME

PAGE 76: WHAT NEXT?

A: B: C:

PAGE 78: SHADOW MATCH

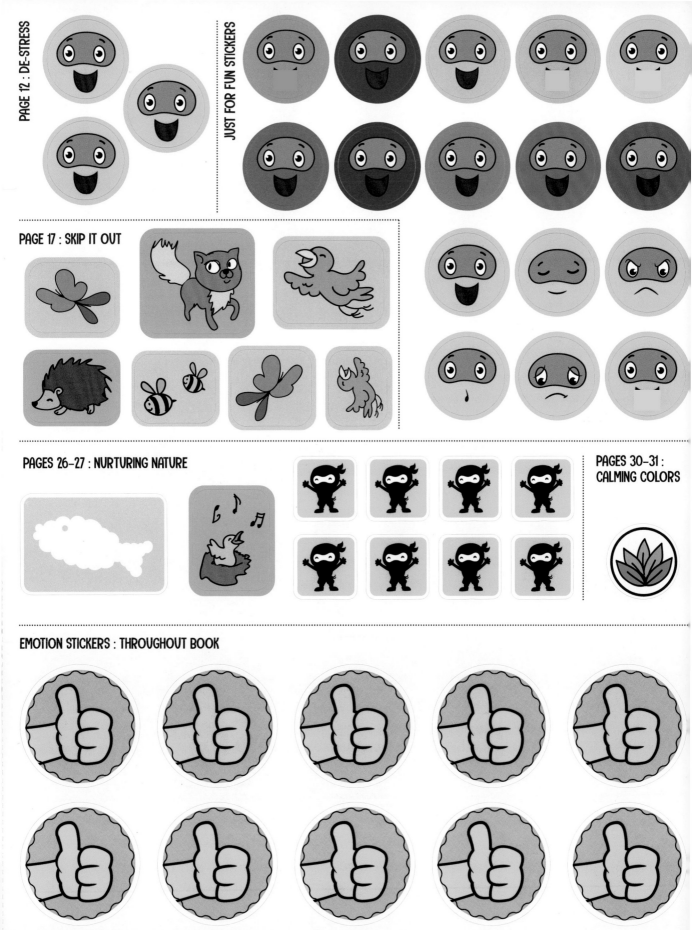

PAGE 12 : DE-STRESS

JUST FOR FUN STICKERS

PAGE 17 : SKIP IT OUT

PAGES 26-27 : NURTURING NATURE

PAGES 30-31 : CALMING COLORS

EMOTION STICKERS : THROUGHOUT BOOK

PAGE 35 : PEACE AT LAST

PAGE 38 : HUG IT OUT!

PAGES 48-49 : MAKE IT MATCH

PAGES 42-43 : SPOT THE DIFFERNCE

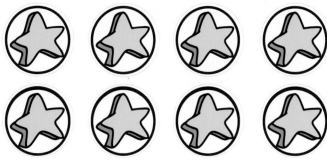

PAGE 64 : PICTURE PERFECT

EMOTION STICKERS : THROUGHOUT BOOK

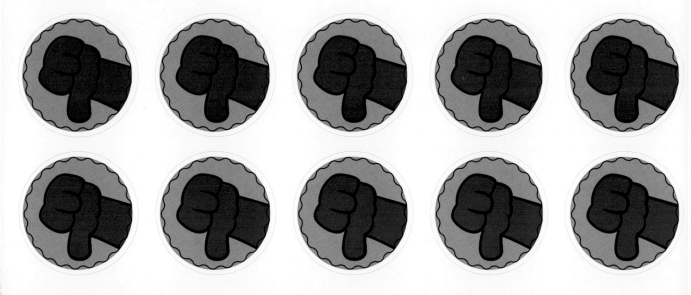